HOW TO SURVIVE 40

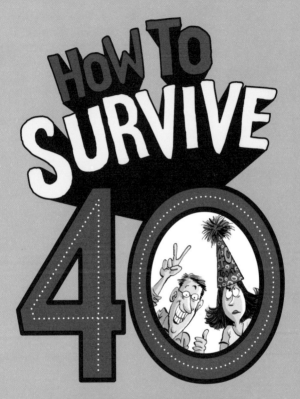

MIKE HASKINS AND CLIVE WHICHELOW
ILLUSTRATIONS BY IAN BAKER

summersdale

HOW TO SURVIVE 40

Summersdale Publishers Ltd
46 West Street
Chichester
West Sussex
PO19 1RP
UK

www.summersdale.com

Printed and bound in China

ISBN: 978-1-84953-935-7

Substantial discounts on bulk quantities of Summersdale books are available to corporations, professional associations and other organisations. For details contact Nicky Douglas by telephone: +44 (0) 1243 756902, fax: +44 (0) 1243 786300 or email: nicky@summersdale.com.

To...................................

From............................

INTRODUCTION

It's a funny old age, 40, isn't it? You're not that old, but then you're not that young either. To teenagers you'll be seen as an old fuddy-duddy who has terrible taste in music, and to older people you'll be seen as some young upstart who has terrible taste in music.

You can't win, which is why you need survival skills. We're not talking Bear Grylls here, although the grizzly one is himself on the wrong side of 40, so he may know a thing or two about it.

No, 40 is the age where you start to defy the ageing process: you refuse to give in, you balk at baldness, you fly in the face of flab and you do something starting with a silent 'w' at wrinkles.

Forty schmorty!

WHY 40 IS DIFFERENT FROM 30

At 30, Mother Nature hadn't started
with the practical jokes – those first grey
hairs and wrinkles were yet to come!

• • • • • • • • • •

You can't have gravitas at 30 – even
if you do have a beard! By 40,
you've earned a bit of respect

• • • • • • • • • •

People who were just starting secondary
school when you hit 30 have now left school,
gone through further education and got
jobs – sometimes better paid than yours!

At 40, the consequences of doing the things you used to enjoy when you were 30 will haunt you for the next decade

REALISTIC AND UNREALISTIC GOALS IN YOUR NEW LIFE AS A 40-YEAR-OLD

REALISTIC GOAL	UNREALISTIC GOAL
To become fit enough to run a marathon	To become fit enough to win Olympic gold at the marathon
To keep up with any new technology Silicon Valley can throw at you	To remember all the passwords you need to actually use the stuff
To become more proficient at DIY so you can fix a few things around the house	To become more proficient at DIY so you can build an entire new house
To learn a new language	To learn how to speak teenager – you get me, fam?

HOW TO PROVE THERE'S PLENTY OF LIFE IN YOU YET

Cycle everywhere – though maybe
not to do the weekly grocery shop

. . . .

Use your jogging bottoms for jogging,
not for lounging on the sofa

. . . .

Start the day with a cold shower –
even if it's just because someone
switched the tap on downstairs

Go to a big music festival
– or at least watch it on
the telly while camping
in the back garden

FINANCIAL OUTGOINGS FROM NOW ON (40-YEAR-OLD MEN)

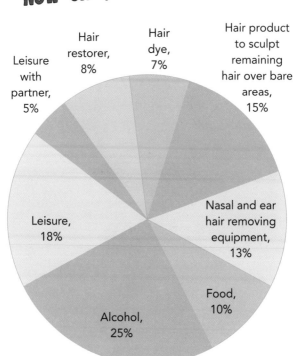

Hair restorer, 8%

Hair dye, 7%

Hair product to sculpt remaining hair over bare areas, 15%

Leisure with partner, 5%

Leisure, 18%

Nasal and ear hair removing equipment, 13%

Food, 10%

Alcohol, 25%

TYPES OF 40-YEAR-OLD YOU COULD BE...

The 40-denier – suddenly begins acting more immaturely than they have ever done before in their life (even when they really were a small child)

. . . .

The prematurely aged 40-year-old – seems to be incredibly relieved that youth is finally over and starts dressing and acting like a pensioner

. . . .

The paranoid 40-year-old who keeps looking at 40-year-old celebs on the internet to see how they've aged compared to them

HOW TO SURVIVE

The desperate 40-year-old who decides this is their last chance to get fit and starts planning their first marathon

EXERCISES FOR 40-YEAR-OLDS

Stretching your memory back
to when you were supple – that
should be pretty vigorous!

. . . .

Touching your toes – OK, you
can sit down if that helps

. . . .

Bending your knees – and yes, that means
unbending them again afterwards, too

. . . .

Pole-dancing – and no, that doesn't mean
a quick foxtrot with your Polish neighbour

REACTIONS THAT 40-YEAR-OLDS MAY INSPIRE IN OTHERS

Wonder – at your slightly manic
over-enthusiasm to join in with
all fun leisure activities

. . . .

Concern – that your slightly manic
over-enthusiasm may quickly
result in heart problems

. . . .

Smugness – although you have more
experience, someone younger will likely
have more hair and a smaller waist

How To
SURVIVE

Amazement – from
teenagers who can't believe
you have reached this
grand age and are still able
to talk without dribbling

WHAT THE TYPICAL 40-YEAR-OLD EATS

Vitamin tablets,
3%

Proper meals you
actually cooked
yourself (includes
use of cook-in
sauce),
5%

Piece of pie,
9%

Sweets, cake,
biscuits you feel
you've earned
after having
healthy stuff,
19%

Ready meals
– because you
didn't have
enough time to
cook something
properly yourself,
38%

Healthy
stuff,
7%

Takeaways –
because you
didn't have
enough time to
do a ready meal,
19%

HOW TO AVOID BEING 40 (EVEN WHEN YOU'RE IN YOUR FORTIES)

Whenever remotely possible,
refuse to act sensibly

. . . .

Stop worrying about your age!

. . . .

Give up, move back in with your ageing
parents and go back to letting them
make all of your life decisions for you

Buck the trend! Get
cosmetic surgery to make
yourself look a bit older!

PEOPLE IT WILL BE INAPPROPRIATE FOR YOU TO HANG OUT WITH

Imaginary friends

• • • • • • • • •

Gangs of kids hanging around in the local town centre (particularly if your own children are among them)

• • • • • • • • •

The rest of the audience at a boy-band concert

YOUR PARENTS —
ESPECIALLY AT A
THEME PARK

A GUIDE TO THE ITEMS THAT A 40-YEAR-OLD MIGHT KEEP IN THE CUPBOARD

ILL-ADVISED	SENSIBLE	OVER-CAUTIOUS
Food products high in saturated fat and cholesterol	Choice of low-fat, low-cholesterol foods	Do-it-yourself liposuction equipment
A stack of takeaway menus	A range of exercise equipment	A portable defibrillator
A pair of rollerblades	A bike	A bike with stabilisers
A book entitled *A Beginner's Guide to Hedge Funds*	A book entitled *A Beginner's Guide to Investment*	A giant piggy bank

BASIC LESSONS TO REMEMBER

If your parents like your new outfit,
go back to the shop for a refund

. . . .

None of us are getting any younger
– but the age at which you start
getting more childish is up to you

. . . .

Your body will become increasingly
reluctant to cooperate with the things
your mind wants to get up to

There's nothing worse than a 40-year-old trying to dress and act like a teenager, apart from, of course, a 50-year-old trying to dress and act like a teenager

THOUGHTS THAT WILL CAUSE YOU UNNECESSARY STRESS

Being 30 only seemed about five minutes ago, so your fiftieth birthday will be here in a flash

· · · · · · · · · ·

Your body reached its peak physical fitness over a decade ago – you're now on the wrong side of the bell curve!

· · · · · · · · · ·

Not only are you not as good-looking as the latest Hollywood heart-throb, you're not as good-looking as yourself a year ago

· · · · · · · · · ·

If they don't market personal jetpacks soon, your joints will not allow you to enjoy them when they finally appear

HOW TO KNOCK A FEW YEARS OFF

Remember that you have only
been an adult for 22 years!

. . . .

Forget the individual years – why
worry about the details? You
are only four in decades

. . . .

Deduct all time spent sleeping or going to
the toilet – this will account for an increasing
percentage of your time as the years go on

Console yourself with
the fact that any years
before the launch of
Facebook can be written
off as there will be little
evidence you existed

WISHES YOU MIGHT ASK OF A GENIE

To look young again – although
preferably without the acne

. . . .

To have your previously clear
memory restored – at least you
think it used to be clear

. . . .

To become irresistible to the opposite sex –
and that doesn't mean by being turned into
either a pint of beer or a bar of chocolate

. . . .

To be filled full of energy again – but
without having to be plugged into the mains

SCIENTIFIC FACTS

You are only 40 because you were born
on time. If you'd been born a little bit
late you'd technically still be in your
thirties or, with a little more discomfort
for your mother, your twenties

• • • • • • • • • •

If you'd been born 1,000 years ago,
40 would have represented your entire
life expectancy – so be thankful!

• • • • • • • • • •

Now, thanks to modern medical advances,
you will be able to enjoy watching yourself
go downhill over the next few decades

You are only 40 because you happen to live on a planet that goes around the sun once every 365 days. If you lived on Uranus you'd be less than six months old!

WHAT YOU WILL BE DOING IN 10 YEARS' TIME

Trying to pass yourself off as someone
who is still in their forties

. . . .

Looking at pictures of yourself when you
were 40 and thinking how young you looked

. . . .

Wondering where the hell a
whole decade went

. . . .

Finally being happy that your waist size
is indisputably smaller than your age

ACTIVITIES THAT WILL NOW CAUSE YOU TO PUT YOUR BACK OUT

Taking your top off at the doctor's in preparation for a routine health check

• • • • • • • • • •

Picking up an unexpectedly heavy book entitled *How to Avoid Back Pain*

• • • • • • • • • •

Massaging your partner after they complain they have put their back out

Reaching for the TV
remote control in too
enthusiastic a manner

BAD ROLE MODELS FOR 40-YEAR-OLDS

Well, people who are 30 for a start

• • • • • • • • • •

Glamorous people who have already
retired and are rolling in money

• • • • • • • • • •

People who have readily embraced
middle age and act like pensioners

PEOPLE WHO REFUSE TO GROW OLD GRACEFULLY — SOME OF THE ROLLING STONES HAVE NEARLY REACHED 40 FOR THE SECOND TIME!

MOMENTS WHEN YOU MAY HAVE TO TRY TO CONTROL YOUR TEMPER

When sales people in shopping centres keep asking if you want to make your will

. . . .

When teenagers assume you won't have heard of any of the bands they like

. . . .

When you are turned down for a new job for being simultaneously 'too old' and 'lacking in experience'

. . . .

When you find yourself working for someone who hadn't started school when you started your first job

FANTASIES YOU MAY START HAVING

There has clearly been a miscalculation in the age department somewhere along the line and you demand a recount

. . . .

Your life to date has in fact been a TV reality show watched by legions of your adoring fans

. . . .

Your partner, offspring and parents will one day tell you that, despite everything they said at the time, you were right about everything all along

This is all just a scary dream
and you will soon wake up
again as an 18-year-old

LESS IMPORTANT AND MORE IMPORTANT THINGS YOU MAY START WORRYING ABOUT

LESS IMPORTANT TO WORRY ABOUT	MORE IMPORTANT TO WORRY ABOUT
You feel bloated after eating	Everyone leaves the room when your bloating starts to ease
You find it difficult to do a three-mile jog	You find it difficult to remember your way home after a three-mile jog
Your fashion sense is a bit behind the times	Strangers think you must be in the middle of filming a costume drama
You are beginning to get baffled by some new technology	You haven't even had a piece of toast for three years since someone gave you a 'smart toaster'

GOOD ROLE MODELS FOR 40-YEAR-OLDS

Mature students who go to university when they're 45 and have the time of their lives

. . . .

Tracey Emin – she is still considered a wild child in some quarters

. . . .

People who still act as if they are in their thirties

Over-forties who appear in adverts for medical products for the ageing – if nothing else, they demonstrate a way in which you can turn your physical decline to your financial advantage

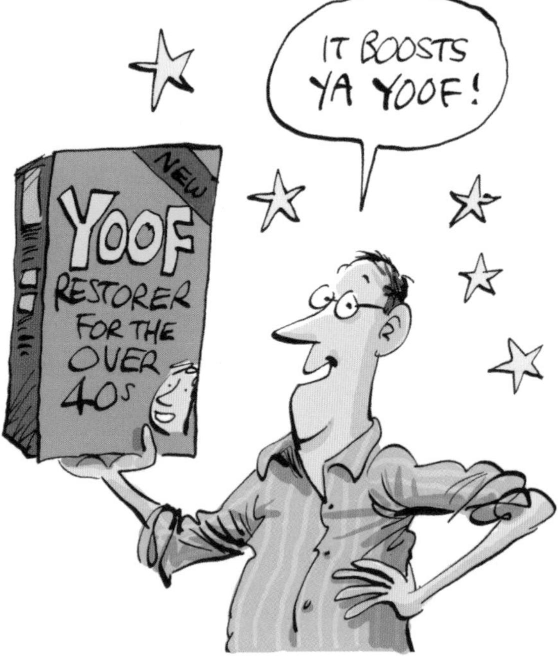
IT BOOSTS YA YOOF!
NEW
YOOF
RESTORER FOR THE OVER 40s

FINANCIAL OUTGOINGS FROM NOW ON (40-YEAR-OLD WOMEN)

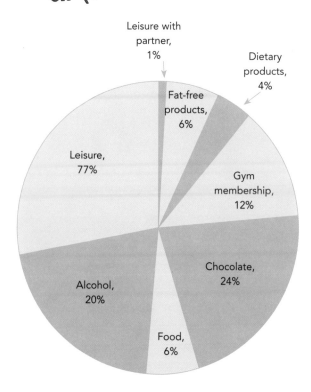

Your hair starts to turn grey – but at least you still have hair to go grey!

. . . .

You feel twinges in your joints when you do anything strenuous – but most sportsmen have had to retire by the time they are your age so you can feel a little bit smug

. . . .

Your waistline starts to expand – but this could save you money by holding your trousers up without the need for a belt

You have to go the toilet more frequently – but jogging back and forth may well provide much-needed extra exercise and as time goes on you may need to get there increasingly quickly

FIRST-DAY DISASTERS

Waking up with a terrible hangover
and the memory of a horrible
dream in which you'd hit 40

· · · · · · · · · ·

Sitting around waiting for 'life to
begin' as you'd been promised

· · · · · · · · · ·

Thinking that if you're still single you'd
better marry the first person who
says yes – even if it's the postman

· · · · · · · · · ·

Deciding today's the day to cash
in your pension and retire

SELF-HELP BOOKS YOU MIGHT WANT TO READ

How Not to Dress Like Your Parents

. . . .

Think Yourself Younger

. . . .

Achieve Greater Self-Esteem by Seeking Out Low-Achieving Former Schoolmates

Do-It-Yourself Hair Transplants Using Tufts from Other Parts of Your Body

ALTERNATIVES TO COSMETIC SURGERY FOR 40-YEAR-OLDS

Stand further and further away from people so they only ever see you in the distance

. . . .

Stand further and further away from the mirror when appraising your wonderful and still-youthful body

. . . .

Blow out your cheeks to make your wrinkles disappear – although this is difficult to sustain all day and you will look like a hamster

COVER A
MULTITUDE OF SINS
WITH A ONESIE —
ESPECIALLY IF
IT HAS A BIT
THAT GOES OVER
YOUR HEAD

WANTED AND UNWANTED NEW FRIENDS

WANTED	UNWANTED
Older people who make you look younger	Very well-preserved 40-year-olds
Gym owners who give mates rates	Gym owners who keep commenting on how out of shape you are
Neighbours who are willing to come round and offer a helping hand	Neighbours who keep coming round to help themselves to the stuff in your house
A boss who recognises you as just the sort of person the business needs	A boss who recognises you as just the sort of person the business could get rid of to make efficiency savings

THINGS 40-YEAR-OLDS PROBABLY SHOULDN'T STILL BE DOING

Wheelies on your bike – well at
least not when anyone's looking

. . . .

Snogging in front of everyone on the
bus – particularly if you are the driver

. . . .

A paper round as your main
source of income

Sending out naked pics
of yourself – particularly
as your personalised
Christmas card design

EMOTIONAL RESPONSES YOU SHOULD PRACTISE AS A 40-YEAR-OLD

EVENT	APPROPRIATE RESPONSE	INAPPROPRIATE RESPONSE
Your partner is contacted by an ex-lover via social media	Laugh it off	Smash the computer up with a sledgehammer
You are told you are being made redundant	Find another job with better money and have a nice holiday with your golden handshake	Make a wax effigy of your boss and stick pins in it
Your loyal old family pet dies	Comfort your partner and children who will be understandably upset	Gather them round to watch while you attempt to flush it down the toilet – this is particularly ill-advised with dogs and cats
Your partner of many years leaves you	You wait for your broken heart to mend before moving on with your life	You dance around the living room singing, 'I thought they'd never go' before organising public auditions for their replacement in the local church hall

LIFESTYLE CHANGES FOR 40-YEAR-OLDS

One of your main leisure-time activities
is now driving other members of your
family to their leisure-time activities

. . . .

You have begun to take pride in
the amount of recycling you do

. . . .

You now feel it's no longer
appropriate to get your dad round
every time any DIY needs doing

HOW TO SURVIVE

You suddenly realise that there's a trade-off between comfort and fashion when choosing new clothes

THINGS THAT 40-YEAR-OLDS DO THAT MAY CONFUSE YOUNG PEOPLE

Reminisce about things that you think happened five years ago, but which in fact happened before they were born

• • • • • • • • • •

Refer to the period 30 years ago as 'the golden age of computer games'

• • • • • • • • • •

Insist on using the phone to contact them rather than just texting – and sometimes, even worse, insisting on using the landline phone

• • • • • • • • • •

Refer to yourself as though you are still young, rather than extraordinarily ancient

Become a 'bright young thing'

· · · · · · · · · ·

Become a millionaire by the time you're 30

· · · · · · · · · ·

Persuade your friends to start calling you
by a cool nickname of your own devising

Be recognised as a child
prodigy – or even a 39-year-old
prodigy, for that matter

THINGS YOU USED TO BE ABLE TO DO THAT NOW SEEM DIFFICULT

THING THAT IS BECOMING DIFFICULT TO DO	SUITABLE EXCUSE
Fit into something you haven't worn for a while	'It must have shrunk while it was hanging up in the wardrobe'
Read the small print in instruction manuals	'It's probably all in Chinese anyway'
Be able to catch all the dialogue in films	'These young actors just mumble all the time'
Get breathless running for the bus	'Global warming has caused the route to the bus stop to expand so it is further away than it used to be'

THINGS IT'S NOT TOO LATE TO DO

Play the lottery – in the vain hope that at least you'll be a millionaire in your forties

. . . .

Grow old disgracefully

. . . .

Become an ageing eccentric

Donate your body to
science so at least someone
will be interested in
seeing you naked again

THINGS TO KEEP TELLING YOURSELF

'I still look good enough to get away with lying about my age'

• • • • • • • • • •

'If I had been born on 29 February I would now only be celebrating my tenth birthday'

• • • • • • • • • •

'I will not succumb to middle-aged spread, baldness or milky malted bedtime drinks'

'BY THE TIME
I'M OLD, THEY'LL
PROBABLY HAVE
FOUND A CURE FOR
BEING OLD'

HOW TO MAINTAIN ENTHUSIASM

Make a list of all the people you know who are even older than you – and always will be!

. . . .

Convince yourself that people in their thirties are a bunch of know-nothings who are still wet behind the ears

. . . .

Remember you are the perfect age to outrun everyone older than yourself and outsmart everyone younger

. . . .

If you catch yourself thinking 'it's all downhill from here', that must mean you're currently on the top of the hill!

Being reluctant to try new experiences – although you may still prefer new experiences that are a little bit like some of your old experiences

. . . .

Not being able to stay out all night long any more – although this may be because you've forgotten where you left your keys

. . . .

Suddenly taking up wearing 'sensible' clothes

Suddenly taking up golf and
wearing ridiculous clothes

THE 40-YEAR-OLD'S 24-HOUR CYCLE

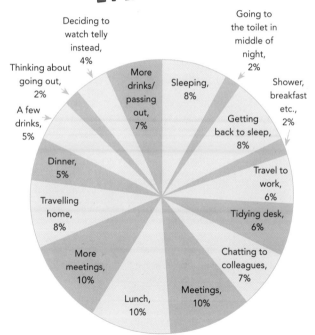

Deciding to watch telly instead, 4%

Going to the toilet in middle of night, 2%

Thinking about going out, 2%

Shower, breakfast etc., 2%

A few drinks, 5%

More drinks/ passing out, 7%

Sleeping, 8%

Getting back to sleep, 8%

Dinner, 5%

Travelling home, 8%

Travel to work, 6%

Tidying desk, 6%

More meetings, 10%

Chatting to colleagues, 7%

Lunch, 10%

Meetings, 10%

WAYS IN WHICH YOUR PARTNER MAY NOW BECOME A DANGER TO YOUR HEALTH

They still expect to sit on your shoulders to watch the headline act at a music festival

. . . .

They become your 24/7 personal unqualified medical and dietary adviser

. . . .

They start asking you to do jobs around the house that paid workmen are prevented from doing because of health and safety regulations

They draw up a bucket
list of hair-raising things
like parachute jumps to
do before you're too old

MEASURES OF SUCCESS

BASIC	ADVANCED
Reaching 40 without looking your age	Reaching 40 and still paying half fare on the bus
Keeping physically fit	Starring in your own workout videos on YouTube
Enjoying an active social life	Enjoying an active social life that doesn't threaten to foreshorten your physical life
Still looking OK when you see yourself in the mirror	Still looking OK when you see yourself in the mirror, even if you're wearing your glasses at the time

Bending down to pick up your dog's
poo causes you a lasting injury

. . . .

Due to your increasingly poor
eyesight you fail to spot that the cat
is asleep on the third stair down

. . . .

You absent-mindedly mistake your stick-
insect collection for a tasty bowl of Twiglets

HOW TO SURVIVE

Your parrot loudly repeats
the rude comments
you mutter behind
your partner's back

CHANGES THAT MAY OCCUR IN YOUR APPEARANCE DURING YOUR FORTIES

NORMAL	NOT SO NORMAL
Your hair starts turning grey and falling out	Other parts of your body start turning grey and falling out
Appearance of crow's feet beside your eyes	Appearance of crow's feet where your feet used to be
Your expanding stomach has been the subject of some comments by friends	Your stomach now has its own Twitter account
You start wearing more sensible clothes	Even your parents are embarrassed to be seen in public with you

SURVIVAL EQUIPMENT THAT 40-YEAR-OLDS SHOULD INVEST IN

A street map of your town with all the public conveniences clearly marked

• • • • • • • • • •

A belt with an alarm that goes off when your waist starts to expand

• • • • • • • • • •

Access to full current psychological profiles for any old flames who seek you out online

• • • • • • • • • •

Emergency medical supplies kit containing hair dye and Botox

THINK POSITIVE!

Now if you think the above heading
should read 'think positively' you're
a proper 40-year-old. If you didn't
notice or don't care then you're still
thinking like a thirty-something

. . . .

'Considering I've drunk enough alcohol to
float the QE2, I'm lucky to be here at all!'

. . . .

'I am younger than more than
50 per cent of the population'

'I'M A 30-YEAR-OLD TRAPPED IN A 40-YEAR-OLD'S BODY — AND AT THIS AGE I'M JUST BEGINNING TO FEEL GRATEFUL FOR THAT EXTRA LAYER OF INSULATION'

If you're interested in finding out more about our books, find us on Facebook at **Summersdale Publishers** and follow us on Twitter at **@Summersdale**.

www.summersdale.com